P9-DHQ-526

Columbus Public Library
2504 14th Street
Columbus NE 68601
402-564-7116

J 001.64 Ra
Raatma, Lucia.
Social networks
33078000517083

21st Century Skills **INNOVATION** *Library*

Social Networks

by Lucia Raatma

Published in the United States of America by Cherry Lake Publishing
Ann Arbor, Michigan
www.cherrylakepublishing.com

Content Adviser: James Commons

Design: The Design Lab

Photo Credits: Cover and pages 1 and 16, ©David J. Green - lifestyle themes/Alamy; page 4,
©iStockphoto.com/vgajic; page 5, ©iStockphoto.com/margotpics; page 6, ©Darko Novakovic,
used under license from Shutterstock, Inc.; page 9, ©iStockphoto.com/MichaelShivers;
page 10, ©iStockphoto.com/ntzolov; page 11, ©TheProductGuy/Alamy; pages 12 and 20,
©Jochen Tack/Alamy; pages 14 and 17, ©ICP/Alamy; page 18, ©iStockphoto.com/Elenathewise;
page 21, ©iStockphoto.com/pkline; page 23, ©iStockphoto.com/gbh007; page 25, ©Justin
Leighton/Alamy; page 26, ©Per Karlsson - BKWine.com/Alamy; page 27, ©AP Images/Khalid
Mohammed; page 29, ©AP Images/Paul Sakuma

Copyright ©2010 by Cherry Lake Publishing
All rights reserved. No part of this book may be reproduced or utilized in any form or by any means
without written permission from the publisher.

Library of Congress Cataloging-in-Publication Data
Raatma, Lucia.
 Social networks / by Lucia Raatma.
    p. cm.–(Innovation in entertainment)
Includes index.
ISBN-13: 978-1-60279-636-2
ISBN-10: 1-60279-636-X
1. Social networks. I. Title.
HM741.R33 2010
006.7'54–dc22   2009027075

Cherry Lake Publishing would like to acknowledge
the work of The Partnership for 21st Century Skills.
Please visit www.21stcenturyskills.org for more information.

Printed in the United States of America
Corporate Graphics Inc.
January 2010
CLSP06

CONTENTS

CHAPTER ONE

The Start of Social Networking

Many people use social networking sites such as MySpace and Facebook to chat or share pictures.

What are your friends up to? Millions of people log on to Facebook each day to find out. Members keep their friends informed of their plans, their activities, their thoughts, and anything else that might be going on.

Facebook is one example of a social network site (SNS), sometimes called a social network service.

Social networking sites have become one of the most popular ways to enjoy the Internet.

On SNSs, users share information. Some details are as simple as what people had for dinner. Other information might be about their favorite places or their movie recommendations. SNSs provide places for people to stay in touch with their friends and family. But where did SNSs come from?

In the early days of the Internet, people eagerly took advantage of what was then a new technology—e-mail.

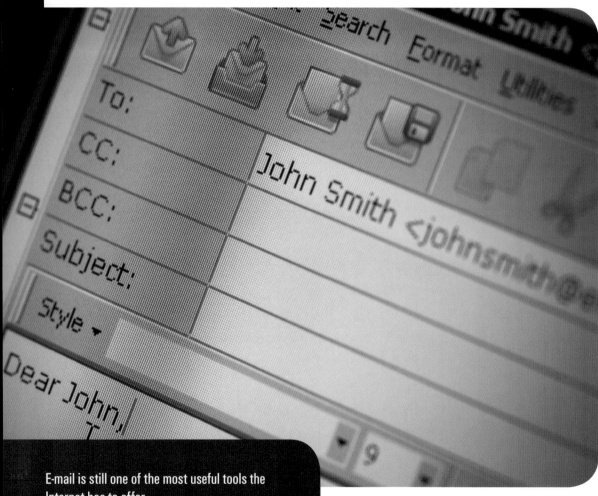

E-mail is still one of the most useful tools the Internet has to offer.

It was a quick way to send a message. Users found it faster than sending a letter. They also often found it more convenient than making a phone call. But e-mail has its limitations. Some Internet users wanted to connect with many people at once. To do that, bulletin board systems (BBS) were created.

Today, MySpace, Facebook, and LinkedIn are well-known sites. Many other SNSs came before them. In the early days, sites such as GeoCities encouraged social networking through **chat rooms**. Then sites began to help people link to one another by using their e-mail addresses. One such site is Classmates.com, which was launched in 1995. Members are encouraged to sign up to get in touch with old schoolmates. The service was like an instant class reunion. The site is still active today and has about 40 million members.

Another early SNS was SixDegrees. It was started in 1997 as a place for people to connect. The site was one of the first to combine many of the features found in today's SNSs. It sent e-mail updates to members about what their friends were doing. People could join groups with others who had similar interests. The site also included "bulletin boards" for members to send short messages to each other. SixDegrees was created so that people could connect not only with existing friends, but also with friends of their friends. But the Internet was

Learning & Innovation Skills

What do you think is the most effective way of communicating with someone? Do you enjoy writing long e-mails to your uncle or grandmother or best friend? Or do you like to pick up the phone? Maybe you enjoy keeping in touch with everyone on an SNS. When do you think it is important to talk face-to-face?

still new, and SixDegrees did not have enough regular users. The site closed in 2000.

One of the first social networking sites created specifically for business users was Ryze, which was launched in 2001. This site encouraged business owners and other professionals to communicate. Other business sites such as Tribe.net and LinkedIn followed. Soon people from all kinds of industries could connect with one another and share information.

In 2002, Friendster was launched. Much like SixDegrees, Friendster was designed to help people connect with the friends of people they knew. Membership grew quickly, but the site experienced technical difficulties and had trouble keeping up. Many users became frustrated and left the site. The company worked to improve the site, and it is still very popular in parts of Asia.

In the next few years, sites such as MySpace, Bebo, and Facebook hit the Internet. Soon sites were available all over the globe in many different languages. Today, millions of people use SNSs to stay in touch.

CHAPTER TWO

Online Innovations

Before computers were popular, a person's social network was fairly simple. It was made up of family and friends from the neighborhood, work, or school. People often wrote and mailed letters, but it might be days or weeks before they would get an answer. They could also call one another. But years ago, long-distance calling was very expensive. It was easy to lose touch with old friends or people who lived far away.

Regular mail used to be one of the few ways to keep in touch with friends or family members who lived far away.

The Internet changed all that. First, e-mail allowed people to write each other—and get nearly instant answers. Then chat rooms and instant messaging (IM) enabled people to write and receive messages almost as quickly as in a spoken conversation. Now, with SNSs, people can stay in touch with a huge group of friends at once. People are able to know what all their friends are doing every day.

Instant messaging makes it easy to chat with friends from the comfort of your home.

Many people use mobile devices, such as the iPod Touch, to check Facebook and other social network sites.

On most SNSs, two users are listed as friends only after both have approved it. Then they are able to see each other's profiles. A user's profile usually includes a name,

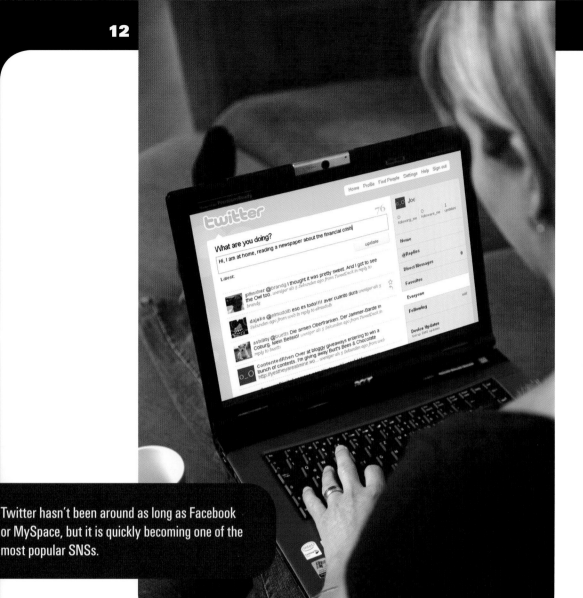

Twitter hasn't been around as long as Facebook or MySpace, but it is quickly becoming one of the most popular SNSs.

birth date, interests, and other details. Users can post photos and write updates about their lives. They can also comment on the posts that their friends make.

Some features have changed as SNSs have improved their formats. For instance, some profiles are private and some are public. Public profiles can be viewed by anyone, not just friends. Also, when users change their information, those details can be made public or kept private. When profiles or details are made private, only a few select people can see the information.

A big innovation in the SNS world is a service called Twitter. Twitter uses a feature called **micro-blogging** to help connect members. This service allows users to send messages called tweets. These are short posts that can be no more than 140 characters in length. Tweets are delivered to a user's followers. Followers are people who sign up to receive another user's updates. Other users can also search for tweets on a certain subject or written by a certain person. Tweets are often sent from cell phones. Some tweets are about everyday things: "I'm stuck in traffic!" Others might be about historic events: "I'm watching the president give a speech." These messages can keep people connected 24 hours a day.

21st Century Content

In 2009, the country of Iran held a presidential election. When the government announced the winner, many people did not believe the outcome. They thought that the election had been unfair. They believed that their votes had not been counted or that the government had stolen the election. People took to the streets to protest. Twitter messages were sent from all over the world to talk about what was happening.

CHAPTER THREE

Keeping in Touch

Who can join an SNS? Just about anyone! Most sites are free, and they appeal to people from all backgrounds.

On most sites, a user creates a profile. Then the site may suggest friends, based on the user's profile information. For example, the site might list people who have the same hobbies or interests as the user. Soon, friends suggest other friends. Users can

Sites such as MySpace allow users to easily create long lists of online friends.

also search for people they have lost touch with. From there, users can post their thoughts every day or every week—whatever suits them. They can also post photos. Their friends can leave comments and offer more ideas.

Besides making friends, SNS users can become fans of organizations that have pages on the SNS. Love baseball? You can be a fan of your local team. Love to cook? Many cooking magazines have pages, too.

SNS users can also have fun with **gadgets** and **applications**. With some applications, friends can send each other virtual gifts. Other applications allow users to take quizzes and challenge their friends to take them, too.

Many SNSs are specialized. For instance, CafeMom is designed for moms. They can log on to ask questions and give one another advice. Many users also **blog** about parenting issues.

On Taltopia, artists can network. Painters, musicians, dancers, actors, and all sorts of performers can communicate with fans. They can also get the attention of industry professionals.

MySpace is a general SNS, but it has proved popular with musicians. They can use it to upload their music for people to hear. This practice has led to many musicians being discovered.

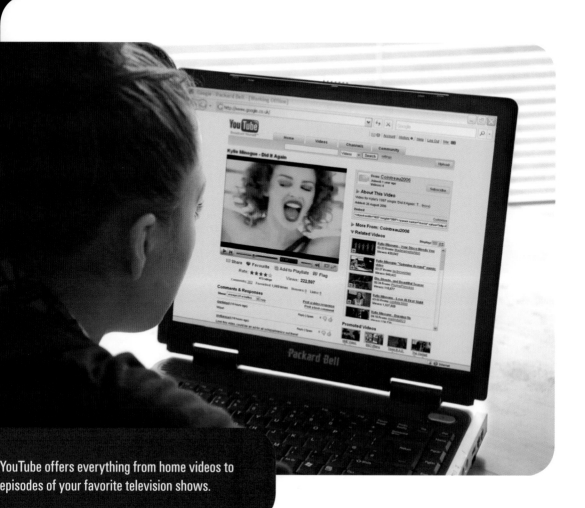

YouTube offers everything from home videos to episodes of your favorite television shows.

On Flickr, people share photos. Users organize their photos by using **tags**. Then other people can use **keywords** to search for images more easily. The photos can be stored in collections that are either public or private. YouTube is a lot like Flickr, except that it allows people to post and share videos instead of photos. Flickr

LinkedIn is a good example of a way social networking can be used for more than just having a good time.

and YouTube did not start out as traditional SNSs but have added social networking features to their sites.

LinkedIn offers networking to people in business. It also helps people who are looking for a job. People can share advice with one another and talk about job openings and other opportunities.

TravBuddy and Travellerspoint are designed for people who like to travel. Users offer information about their favorite vacation spots. They post photos and blogs.

Your parents can help you find social networking sites that are safe for kids to use.

They can even find travel buddies. Shelfari helps book lovers connect and share recommendations.

On many sites, users must be a certain age in order to join. For instance, Facebook and MySpace require that users be at least 13 years old. However, there are a number of sites designed especially for kids. Kid-friendly sites include Whyville, Webkinz, and Club Penguin. Whyville is free, and users earn play money by playing educational games. At Webkinz, kids register stuffed animals they have bought. Then they can play games, earn points, and buy items for their pets. There are also chat rooms for users. On Club Penguin, users have to pay a fee to join. Then they design penguin **avatars** and play games. These three sites boast that their chat rooms are safe for kids.

SNSs have much to offer people. They have allowed users all over the world to connect and stay in touch.

21st Century Content

It can be fun to create a profile on an SNS. You might also enjoy talking to new friends in a chat room. But sharing too much information can be dangerous. Telling people where you live or go to school is risky. It is best to keep that information off the Internet. Strangers may contact you and want to meet. If a stranger asks to meet or says anything that makes you feel uncomfortable, always tell an adult.

CHAPTER FOUR

The Future of SNSs

Social networking has become an everyday activity for millions of people around the world.

Social network sites have a fairly short history. Still, a lot has changed in a few years. By some reports, Facebook has more than 300 million users. Twitter membership grew 3,000 percent between 2008 and 2009. So what will happen in the years to come? Where are SNSs headed?

Some people believe that there are too many SNSs. In order to keep up with friends on Twitter, you

It can be easy to end up spending too much time online if you have profiles on many different sites.

have to join that service. But what about your sister on Facebook? And your best friend on MySpace? Keeping track of everyone would mean having a profile on all of these sites. Many people do not have time to maintain more than one profile. The answer may be a single login that will connect users to all the sites at once.

Life & Career Skills

Have you ever been bullied by anyone at school? There are bullies online, too. Some SNS users have posted terrible stories or photos of other people that are hurtful or that they made up. This is serious, and a lot of people can be hurt. How would you feel if someone posted an embarrassing photo of you? Or spread lies about you? Think twice before you put anything on the Internet.

Some companies are working on developing new technology to link several SNSs together. Already, Facebook has created some connection options. For instance, if you post a video on YouTube, you can share it on Facebook, too.

In 2009, Google introduced Google Wave. The system supports both documents and conversation. Google Wave is a format for real-time messages and sharing photos, videos, and more. Conversations, or "waves," will also connect to other sites. Who knows where technology like this will take SNSs?

Most people agree that the majority of SNSs will remain free for users. Sites, however, may feature more and more advertising. Many companies hope that placing their products on SNSs will be profitable. Time will tell how successful this type of advertising will be for companies.

SNSs may also be affected by lifestreaming. The lifestreaming format is similar to a blog. It can have photos, videos, comments, posts, and other information.

Many businesses have started using SNSs as ways to advertise their products to young people.

Lifestreaming combines a person's blog posts with information from an SNS profile. It also includes the user's photos and videos from sites such as YouTube and Flickr. Some lifestream formats scroll horizontally instead of vertically. These formats can look like a timeline of a person's life.

Not everyone is in favor of SNSs. Some critics say that people give out too much information on SNSs. Users talk about unimportant events and spend too much time online. They take quizzes and make lists. They urge their friends to do the same. Some critics cannot understand why anyone would want to send tweets all day. It seems like a waste of time to them.

Some users get tired of posting and reading comments. They find they want to spend time with friends in person, not just on a computer. Some also think that Twitter is too much trouble to use—or just not necessary.

Many people think SNSs are great and that they are here to stay. Fans of SNSs seem to enjoy chatting with one another on a regular basis. The technology may change over and over. Who knows what users will be able to do in the years ahead? No matter what, most people believe that SNSs will remain important sources of information and communication.

CHAPTER FIVE

SNS Innovators

A number of people have played a part in the evolution of SNSs. Here are just a few who have made their marks online.

Tim Berners-Lee (1955–) is credited with inventing the World Wide Web. He is a computer scientist and professor. He worked with **hypertext** as a way to share information. He designed and built the first Web browser, Web server, and

Tim Berners-Lee paved the way for the many Internet applications we use today.

Web site. His work made the creation of SNSs and blogs possible.

Reid Hoffman (1967–) is a businessman who co-founded LinkedIn. This business networking site helps people connect, especially when they're hunting for jobs. Before creating LinkedIn, he worked for Apple Computer. He also co-founded SocialNet.com, another

Reid Hoffman's work on LinkedIn has helped change the way people use social networking sites.

Jack Dorsey helped create Twitter, a popular online service.

SNS. He has also worked for PayPal, a system that allows people to pay for goods online. He is well known in Silicon Valley, an area in California that has many high-tech companies.

Jack Dorsey (1976–) is a software developer and co-founder of Twitter. As a teenager, he was interested in how companies communicated when they sent out taxis, ambulances, and other services. He created software that made this system more efficient. He knew that IMs

Life & Career Skills

Being ready to take on new challenges is key for any businessperson. Chris Hughes is a good example of that. He helped found Facebook, Inc. while he was a student at Harvard University. He is still a consultant for that company. He made a big impact by heading up a networking site for Barack Obama during the 2008 presidential campaign. My.BarackObama.com helped supporters raise funds, organize rallies, and connect with one another. This idea was groundbreaking. Many people believe this site played an important part in President Obama's election.

and text messaging could be very useful. This knowledge inspired him to find more ways for people to communicate in real time. His ideas led to the launch of Twitter in 2006.

Brad Greenspan is an Internet innovator who was involved in the creation of MySpace. He founded eUniverse in 1998. This was an Internet marketing company. While there, he supervised Tom Anderson (who became president of MySpace) and Chris DeWolfe (who became the head of MySpace). These men and a group of programmers launched MySpace in 2003. Since then, Greenspan has gone on to establish LiveUniverse. This company owns SNS and video companies.

Mark Zuckerberg (1984–) was a student at Harvard University when he created Facebook in 2004. Originally, it was a networking site only for Harvard students. Then,

Mark Zuckerberg created Facebook and is now the company's Chief Executive Officer (CEO).

with the help of others, including his two roommates, Chris Hughes and Dustin Moskovitz, Zuckerberg expanded the service. First it spread to other colleges. Then it spread worldwide. Today, Zuckerberg is the head of Facebook.

Glossary

applications (ap-luh-KAY-shuhnz) computer programs that perform certain tasks

avatars (A-vuh-tarz) electronic images that represent and are controlled by computer users

blog (BLOG) to write bits of text that are posted on the Internet, usually for others to see

chat rooms (CHAT ROOMZ) places on the Web where multiple computer users can communicate in real time

gadgets (GAD-jets) small computer applications that have specific purposes

hypertext (HYE-pur-tekst) a system of storing text, tables, images, and other features with links to related content

keywords (KEE-wurdz) words used to search for information on the Internet

micro-blogging (MY-kroh BLOG-ing) posting short updates about what a person is doing, usually consisting of short text messages

tags (TAGZ) keywords added to a blog post or other set of information making it easier for users to locate information

For More Information

BOOKS

Brown, Anne. *Virtual Danger: Staying Safe Online*. Mankato, MN: Compass Point Books, 2009.

Jakubiak, David J. *A Smart Kid's Guide to Social Networking Online*. New York: PowerKids Press, 2010.

Mooney, Carla. *Online Social Networking*. Detroit: Lucent Books, 2009.

Woog, Adam. *Mark Zuckerberg: Facebook Creator*. Detroit: KidHaven Press, 2009.

WEB SITES

KidsHealth—Your Online Identity
kidshealth.org/kid/watch/house/online_id.html#
Read some good advice about staying safe online.

NetSmartzKids
www.netsmartzkids.org/indexFL.htm
Play games and learn more about Internet safety.

Nicktropolis
www.nick.com/nicktropolis/game/index.jhtml
Play games, chat with friends, and decorate your own room.

Index

About the Author

Lucia Raatma has written dozens of books for young readers. She enjoys keeping in touch with friends and relatives on Facebook. She and her family live in the Tampa Bay area of Florida.